Morning Glory

Prayer Journal

JUANITA BYNUM

Pneuma Life Publishing

Morning Glory Prayer Journal

Unless otherwise noted, Scripture quotations are taken from the King James Version of the Bible.

Printed in the United States of America

Copyright © 1999 Juanita Bynum
Morning Glory Prayer Journal
ISBN 1-56229-156-4

Pneuma Life Publishing
P. O. Box 885
Lanham, Maryland 20703-0885
(301) 577-4052
http://www.pneumalife.com

Design By DesignPoint, Inc.
designpointinc.com

morning glory

Because thy lovingkindness is better than life,
my lips shall praise thee. Psalm 63:3

Be thou my strong habitation, whereunto I may continually resort: thou hast given commandment to save me; for thou art my rock and my fortress. Psalm 71:3

Blessed be the Lord, because he hath heard
the voice of my supplications. Psalm 28:6

But know that the Lord hath set apart him that is godly for himself:
the Lord will hear when I call unto him. Psalm 4:3

I will instruct thee and teach thee in the way which thou
shalt go: I will guide thee with mine eye. Psalm 32:8

His glory is great in Your salvation; Honor and
majesty You have placed upon him. Psalm 21:5

I delight to do thy will, O my God: yea,
thy law is within my heart. Psalm 40:8

*Then will I go unto the altar of God, unto God my exceeding joy:
yea, upon the harp will I praise thee, O God my God. Psalm 43:4*

*Who is this King of glory? The Lord strong and
mighty, The Lord mighty in battle. Psalm 21:7*

Come, let us worship and bow down: let us
kneel before the LORD our maker. Psalm 95:6

*Sing unto the Lord a new song: sing
unto the Lord, all the earth. Psalm 96:1*

prayer journal

Yes, they shall sing of the ways of the Lord,
For great is the glory of the Lord. Psalm 138:5

Oh that men would praise the Lord for his goodness, and for
his wonderful works to the children of men! Psalm 107:8

prayer journal

•

_Let the saints be joyful in glory; Let them
sing aloud on their beds. Psalm 149:5_

_He hath delivered my soul in peace from the battle that was
against me: for there were many with me. Psalm 55:18_

God, thou hast taught me from my youth: and hitherto
have I declared thy wondrous works. Psalm 71:17

_____

_____

_____

_____

_____

_____

_____

_____

_____

_____

_____

_____

_____

_____

_____

_____

_____

_____

_____

_____

_____

*From the rising of the sun unto the going down of the
same the Lord's name is to be praised. Psalm 113:3*

Let my prayer be set forth before thee as incense; and the lifting up of my hands as the evening sacrifice. Psalm 141:2

I will say of the Lord, He is my refuge and my
fortress: my God; in him will I trust. Psalm 91:2

prayer journal

And my tongue shall speak of thy righteousness
and of thy praise all the day long. Psalm 35:28

But God is the judge: he putteth down one,
and setteth up another. Psalm 75:7

Bless the Lord, O my soul: and all that is
within me, bless his holy name. Psalm 103:1

*With the merciful thou wilt shew thyself merciful; with an
upright man thou wilt shew thyself upright. Psalm 18:25*

*My soul is continually in my hand: yet
do I not forget thy law. Psalm 119:109*

Praise ye the Lord. I will praise the Lord with my whole heart, in the assembly of the upright, and in the congregation. Psalm 111:1

I am as a wonder unto many; but
thou art my strong refuge. Psalm 71:7

Exalt ye the LORD our God, and worship
at his footstool; for he is holy. Psalm 99:5

I will praise thee: for thou hast heard me, and
art become my salvation. Psalm 118:21

Let the proud be ashamed; for they dealt perversely with me
without a cause: but I will meditate in thy precepts. Psalm 119:78

I am small and despised: yet do not
I forget thy precepts. Psalm 119:141

*Clap your hands, all ye people; shout unto
God with the voice of triumph. Psalm 47:1*

*Let the redeemed of the Lord say so, whom he hath
redeemed from the hand of the enemy. Psalm 107:2*

They shall speak of the glory of Your kingdom,
And talk of Your power. Psalm 145:11

_I will instruct thee and teach thee in the way which thou
shalt go: I will guide thee with mine eye. Psalm 32:8_

*It is of the LORD'S mercies that we are not consumed, because his compassions fail not.
They are new every morning: great is thy faithfulness. Lamentations 3:22-23*

Seek him that maketh the seven stars and Orion, and turneth the shadow of death into the morning, and maketh the day dark with night: that calleth for the waters of the sea, and poureth them out upon the face of the earth: The LORD is his name. *Amos 5:8*

But his delight is in the law of the Lord; and in his law doth he meditate day and night. Psalm 1:2

Praise ye the Lord. Praise ye the Lord from the
heavens: praise him in the heights. Psalm 148:1

I will sing of mercy and judgment: unto thee, O Lord, will I sing. Psalm 101:1

My mouth shall speak of wisdom; and the meditation
of my heart shall be of understanding. Psalm 49:3

When I remember thee upon my bed, and
meditate on thee in the night watches. Psalm 63:6

I will delight myself in thy statutes:
I will not forget thy word. Psalm 119:16

morning glory

*He sent his word, and healed them, and delivered
them from their destructions. Psalm 107:20*

Praise ye the Lord: for it is good to sing praises unto our God;
for it is pleasant; and praise is comely. Psalm 147:1

They that trust in the LORD shall be as mount Zion,
which cannot be removed, but abideth for ever. Psalm 125:1

Blessed is the man that walketh not in the counsel of the ungodly, nor standeth in the way of sinners, nor sitteth in the seat of the scornful. Psalm 1:1

In God we boast all the day long, and
praise thy name for ever. Selah. Psalm 44:8

prayer journal

Trust in the Lord, and do good; so shalt thou dwell
in the land, and verily thou shalt be fed. Psalm 37:3

*To such as keep his covenant, and to those that remember
his commandments to do them. Psalm 103:18*

*There shall no evil befall thee, neither shall any
plague come nigh thy dwelling. Psalm 91:10*

To the end that my glory may sing praise to You and not be silent.
O Lord my God, I will give thanks to You forever. Psalm 30:12

*I will meditate in thy precepts, and have
respect unto thy ways. Psalm 119:15*

I will praise thee, O Lord my God, with all my heart:
and I will glorify thy name for evermore. Psalm 86:12

_The Lord upholdeth all that fall, and raiseth up all
those that be bowed down._ Psalm 145:14

Bless our God, ye people, and make the voice
of his praise to be heard. Psalm 66:8

Seven times a day do I praise thee because of
thy righteous judgments. Psalm 119:164

Lord, open thou my lips; and my mouth
shall shew forth thy praise. Psalm 51:15

I will praise thee for ever, because thou hast done it: and I will wait on thy name; for it is good before thy saints. Psalm 52:9

_But as for me, my prayer is unto thee, O LORD, in an acceptable time: O God,
in the multitude of thy mercy hear me, in the truth of thy salvation. Psalm 69:13_

So will I sing praise unto thy name for ever,
that I may daily perform my vows. Psalm 61:8

_My hands also will I lift up unto thy commandments, which I
have loved; and I will meditate in thy statutes. Psalm 119:48_

How love I thy law! it is my meditation
all the day. Psalm 119:97

*He hath remembered his covenant for ever, the word which
he commanded to a thousand generations. Psalm 105:8*

But the king shall rejoice in God; Everyone who swears by Him shall glory;
But the mouth of those who speak lies shall be stopped. Psalm 63:11

*Commit thy way unto the Lord; trust also in him;
and he shall bring it to pass. Psalm 37:5*

I have more understanding than all my teachers:
for thy testimonies are my meditation. Psalm 119:99

Lord our Lord, how excellent is thy name in all the earth!
who hast set thy glory above the heavens. Psalm 8:1

He healeth the broken in heart, and
bindeth up their wounds. Psalm 147:3

_By the word of the LORD were the heavens made; and all
the host of them by the breath of his mouth. Psalm 33:6_

*My lips shall utter praise, when thou hast
taught me thy statutes. Psalm 119:171*

The heavens declare the glory of God; And the firmament shows His handiwork. Psalm 19:1

*For he spake, and it was done; he
commanded, and it stood fast. Psalm 33:9*

Lift up your heads, O you gates! And be lifted up, you everlasting doors! And the King of glory shall come in. Psalm 21:6

_Trust in him at all times; ye people, pour out your heart
before him: God is a refuge for us. Selah. Psalm 62:8_

_My covenant will I not break, nor alter the
thing that is gone out of my lips. Psalm 89:34_

*But I will hope continually, and will yet
praise thee more and more. Psalm 71:14*

The law of the Lord is perfect, converting the soul: the testimony
of the Lord is sure, making wise the simple. Psalm 19:7

The Lord GOD hath given me the tongue of the learned, that I should know how to speak a word in season to him that is weary: he wakeneth morning by morning, he wakeneth mine ear to hear as the learned. Isaiah 50:4

Evening, and morning, and at noon, will I pray, and
cry aloud: and he shall hear my voice. Psalm 55:17

*Bless the Lord, O my soul: and all that is within
me, bless his holy name. Psalm 103:1*

LORD, be gracious unto us; we have waited for thee: be thou their arm
every morning, our salvation also in the time of trouble. Isaiah 33:2

Lord my God, I cried unto thee, and
thou hast healed me. Psalm 30:2

All the earth shall worship thee, and shall sing unto thee;
they shall sing to thy name. Selah. Psalm 66:4

But thou, O Lord, art a shield for me; my glory,
and the lifter up of mine head. Psalm 3:3

*I cried unto thee, O Lord: I said, Thou art my refuge and
my portion in the land of the living. Psalm 142:5*

Praise him upon the loud cymbals:praise him
upon the high sounding cymbals. Psalm 150:5

Let them praise the name of the Lord: for his name alone is excellent;
his glory is above the earth and heaven. Psalm 148:13

Thou art my hiding place and my shield:
I hope in thy word. Psalm 119:114

The Lord is my shepherd;
I shall not want. Psalm 23:1

And they rose up in the morning early, and
worshiped before the LORD. 1 Samuel 1:19

The Lord is my strength and my shield; my heart trusted in him, and I am helped: therefore my heart greatly rejoiceth; and with my song will I praise him. Psalm 28:7

I delight to do thy will, O my God: yea,
thy law is within my heart. Psalm 40:8

*Delight thyself also in the Lord; and he shall give
thee the desires of thine heart. Psalm 37:4*

_Judge me, O Lord; for I have walked in mine integrity: I have
trusted also in the Lord; therefore I shall not slide. Psalm 26:1_

My mouth shall speak the praise of the Lord: and let all flesh
bless his holy name for ever and ever. Psalm 145:21

Rest in the Lord, and wait patiently for him: fret not thyself because of him who prospereth in his way, because of the man who bringeth wicked devices to pass. Psalm 37:7

*Sing unto the Lord with thanksgiving; sing praise
upon the harp unto our God. Psalm 147:7*

Wait on the Lord, and keep his way, and he shall exalt thee to inherit the land: when the wicked are cut off, thou shalt see it. Psalm 37:34

The Lord shall judge the people: judge me, O Lord, according to my
righteousness, and according to mine integrity that is in me. Psalm 7:8

Whoso offereth praise glorifieth me: and to him that ordereth his conversation aright will I shew the salvation of God. Psalm 50:23

Salvation belongeth unto the Lord: thy
blessing is upon thy people. Psalm 3:8

Trust in him at all times; ye people, pour out your heart
before him: God is a refuge for us. Psalm 62:8

To shew forth thy lovingkindness in the morning,
and thy faithfulness every night. Psalm 92:2

*I will meditate also of all thy work,
and talk of thy doings. Psalm 77:12*

But I will sing of thy power; yea, I will sing aloud of thy mercy in the morning: for thou hast been my defense and refuge in the day of my trouble. Psalm 59:16

_Taste and see that the LORD is good: blessed
is the man that trusteth in him. Psalm 34:8_

And they that know thy name will put their trust in thee: for thou,
LORD, hast not forsaken them that seek thee. Psalm 9:10

*As the hart panteth after the water brooks, so
panteth my soul after thee, O God. Psalm 42:1*

I will praise thee, O Lord, with my whole heart; I will
shew forth all thy marvellous works. Psalm 9:1

Declare His glory among the nations, His wonders among all peoples. Psalm 96:3

_____

_____

_____

_____

_____

_____

_____

_____

_____

_____

_____

_____

_____

_____

_____

_____

_____

_____

_____

_____

_____

_____

_____

_____

_____

_____

That I may shew forth all thy praise in the gates of the
daughter of Zion: I will rejoice in thy salvation. Psalm 9:14

Be thou exalted, Lord, in thine own strength: so will we sing and praise thy power. Psalm 21:13

God, my heart is steadfast; I will sing and give
praise, even with my glory. Psalm 108:1

Cause me to hear thy lovingkindness in the morning; for in thee do I trust: cause me to know the way wherein I should walk; for I lift up my soul unto thee. Psalm 143:8

*Thy word is true from the beginning:and every one of thy
righteous judgments endureth for ever. Psalm 119:160*

_Why art thou cast down, O my soul? and why art thou disquieted
within me?hope thou in God: for I shall yet praise him,who is the
health of my countenance, and my God. Psalm 42:11_

My heart is fixed, O God, my heart is fixed:
I will sing and give praise. Psalm 57:7

Give ear, O Shepherd of Israel, thou that leadest Joseph like a flock; thou that dwellest between the cherubims, shine forth. Psalm 80:1

And the Lord shall help them and deliver them: he shall deliver them from the wicked, and save them, because they trust in him. Psalm 37:40

Rejoice in the Lord, O ye righteous: for praise
is comely for the upright. Psalm 33:1

Give unto the Lord, O you mighty ones, Give
unto the Lord glory and strength. Psalm 29:1

*Fret not thyself because of evildoers, neither be thou
envious against the workers of iniquity. Psalm 37:1*

Not unto us, O Lord, not unto us, But to Your name give glory,
Because of Your mercy, Because of Your truth. Psalm 115:1

Offer the sacrifices of righteousness, and
put your trust in the LORD. Psalm 4:5

*I will bless the Lord, who hath given me counsel: my
reins also instruct me in the night seasons. Psalm 16:7*

The Lord is my strength and my shield; my heart trusted in him, and I am helped: therefore my heart greatly rejoiceth; and with my song will I praise him. Psalm 28:7

*My mouth shall speak of wisdom; and the meditation
of my heart shall be of understanding. Psalm 49:3*

*And to stand every morning to thank and praise
the LORD, and likewise at even.   1 Chron. 23:30*

Ye that fear the Lord, praise him; all ye the seed of Jacob, glorify him; and fear him, all ye the seed of Israel. Psalm 22:23

But let all those that put their trust in thee rejoice: let them ever shout for joy, because thou defendest them: let them also that love thy name be joyful in thee. Psalm 5:11

But I have trusted in thy mercy; my heart
shall rejoice in thy salvation. Psalm 13:5

*And they remembered that God was their rock,
and the high God their redeemer. Psalm 78:35*

*As for God, his way is perfect: the word of the LORD is tried:
he is a buckler to all those that trust in him. Psalm 18:30*

In thee, O LORD, do I put my trust; let me never be
ashamed: deliver me in thy righteousness. Psalm 31:1

Many sorrows shall be to the wicked: but he that trusteth in
the LORD, mercy shall compass him about. Psalm 32:10

What time I am afraid, I will
trust in thee. Psalm 56:3

*For thou art my rock and my fortress; therefore for
thy name's sake lead me, and guide me. Psalm 31:3*

*Honour and majesty are before him: strength
and beauty are in his sanctuary. Psalm 96:6*

Enter into his gates with thanksgiving, and into his courts with praise: be thankful unto him, and bless his name. Psalm 100:4

Glory in His holy name; Let the hearts of those
rejoice who seek the Lord! Psalm 105:3

My voice shalt thou hear in the morning, O LORD; in the morning
will I direct my prayer unto thee, and will look up. Psalm 5:3

_I waited patiently for the Lord; and he inclined
unto me, and heard my cry. Psalm 40:1_

*Let them praise the name of the Lord; For His name alone is
exalted; His glory is above the earth and heaven. Psalm 148:13*

I will never forget thy precepts: for with them
thou hast quickened me. Psalm 119:93

_Blessed is that man that maketh the LORD his trust, and respecteth
not the proud, nor such as turn aside to lies. Psalm 40:4_

*Let the people praise thee, O God; let all
the people praise thee. Psalm 67:3*

Give to the Lord the glory due His name; Bring an offering, and come into His courts. Psalm 96:8

But the salvation of the righteous is of the Lord: he is
their strength in the time of trouble. Psalm 37:39

Give thanks unto the Lord; for he is good: because
his mercy endureth for ever. Psalm 118:1

Make a joyful noise unto the Lord, all the earth: make a loud noise, and rejoice, and sing praise. Psalm 98:4

My flesh and my heart faileth: but God is the strength of my heart, and my portion for ever. Psalm 73:26

*I will sing of the mercies of the Lord for ever: with my mouth will
I make known thy faithfulness to all generations. Psalm 89:1*

In God I will praise his word, in God I have put my trust;
I will not fear what flesh can do unto me. Psalm 56:4

Great is the Lord, and greatly to be praised in the city of
our God, in the mountain of his holiness. Psalm 48:1

For his anger endureth but a moment; in his favour is life: weeping may endure for a night, but joy cometh in the morning. Psalm 30:5

Let every thing that hath breath praise the
Lord. Praise ye the Lord. Psalm 150:6

Help us, O God of our salvation, For the glory of Your name; And deliver us, and provide atonement for our sins, For Your name's sake! Psalm 79:9

Now know I that the Lord saveth his anointed; he will hear him from
his holy heaven with the saving strength of his right hand. Psalm 20:6

My meditation of him shall be sweet:
I will be glad in the Lord. Psalm 104:34

prayer journal

Because thy lovingkindness is better than life,
my lips shall praise thee. Psalm 63:3

He only is my rock and my salvation; he is my
defense; I shall not be greatly moved. Psalm 62:2

*Praise him with the sound of the trumpet: praise
him with the psaltery and harp. Psalm 150:3*

*Trust in him at all times; ye people, pour out your
heart before him: God is a refuge for us. Psalm 62:8*

The Lord liveth; and blessed be my rock; and let
the God of my salvation be exalted. Psalm 18:46

morning glory

_As for me, I will call upon God; and the
Lord shall save me. Psalm 55:16_

But the salvation of the righteous is of the Lord: he is
their strength in the time of trouble. Psalm 37:39

Surely he shall deliver thee from the snare of the fowler,
and from the noisome pestilence. Psalm 91:3

Unto thee, O my strength, will I sing: for God is my defense, and the God of my mercy. Psalm 59:17

Incline my heart unto thy testimonies,
and not to covetousness. Psalm 119:36

But his delight is in the law of the Lord; and in his
law doth he meditate day and night. Psalm 1:2

What man is he that feareth the Lord? him shall he
teach in the way that he shall choose. Psalm 25:12

I will worship toward thy holy temple, and praise thy name for thy lovingkindness and for thy truth: for thou hast magnified thy word above all thy name. Psalm 138:2

I will praise thee with uprightness of heart, when I shall have learned thy righteous judgments. Psalm 119:7

But You, O Lord, are a shield for me, My glory and the One who lifts up my head. Psalm 3:3

*My soul thirsteth for God, for the living God: when
shall I come and appear before God? Psalm 42:2*

*The righteous shall inherit the land, and
dwell therein for ever. Psalm 37:29*

*I will praise thee with my whole heart: before the
gods will I sing praise unto thee. Psalm 138:1*

My heart is fixed, O God, my heart is fixed:
I will sing and give praise. Psalm 57:7

But the Lord is my defense; and my God
is the rock of my refuge. Psalm 94:22

*Magnify the Lord with me, and let us
exalt his name together. Psalm 34:3*

Blessed is that man that maketh the Lord his trust, and respecteth not the proud, nor such as turn aside to lies. Psalm 40:4

For the Lord God is a sun and shield; The Lord will give grace and glory;
No good thing will He withhold From those who walk uprightly. Psalm 84:11

And call upon me in the day of trouble: I will deliver
thee, and thou shalt glorify me. Psalm 50:15

*Come, let us sing unto the Lord: let us make a
joyful noise to the rock of our salvation. Psalm 95:1*

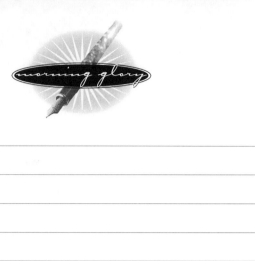

*In God is my salvation and my glory; The rock of
my strength, And my refuge, is in God. Psalm 62:7*

Praise him for his mighty acts: praise him according
to his excellent greatness. Psalm 150:2

The Lord also will be a refuge for the oppressed,
a refuge in times of trouble. Psalm 9:9

And the heavens shall praise thy wonders, O Lord: thy faithfulness also in the congregation of the saints. Psalm 89:5

The righteous shall be glad in the Lord, and trust in Him.
And all the upright in heart shall glory. Psalm 64:10

Thy mercy, O Lord, is in the heavens; and thy faithfulness reacheth unto the clouds. Psalm 36:5

_____

_____

_____

_____

_____

_____

_____

_____

_____

_____

_____

_____

_____

_____

_____

_____

_____

_____

_____

_____

_____

_____

_____

_____

_____

The Lord is my strength and my shield; my heart trusted in him, and I am helped:
therefore my heart greatly rejoiceth; and with my song will I praise him. Psalm 28:7

And now shall mine head be lifted up above mine enemies round
about me: therefore will I offer in his tabernacle sacrifices of joy;
I will sing, yea, I will sing praises unto the Lord. Psalm 27:6

*I hate vain thoughts: but thy law
do I love. Psalm 119:113*

In God is my salvation and my glory: the rock of my
strength, and my refuge, is in God. Psalm 62:7

_Give unto the Lord the glory due to His name; Worship
the Lord in the beauty of holiness. Psalm 29:2_

Stand in awe, and sin not: commune with your
own heart upon your bed, and be still. Psalm 4:4

But unto thee have I cried, O LORD; and in the morning
shall my prayer prevent thee. Psalm 88:13

Yet the LORD will command his lovingkindness in the daytime, and in the night
his song shall be with me, and my prayer unto the God of my life. Psalm 42:8

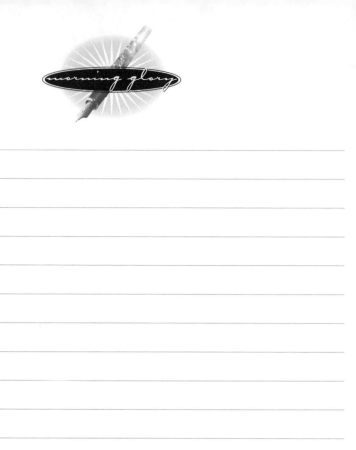

I will sing unto the Lord as long as I live: I will sing
praise to my God while I have my being. Psalm 104:33

*I delight to do thy will, O my God: yea,
thy law is within my heart. Psalm 40:8*

*For he shall deliver the needy when he crieth; the poor
also, and him that hath no helper. Psalm 72:12*

And my tongue shall speak of thy righteousness
and of thy praise all the day long. Psalm 35:28

I cried unto the Lord with my voice, and he
heard me out of his holy hill. Psalm 3:4

I have not departed from thy judgments:
for thou hast taught me. Psalm 119:102

You will guide me with Your counsel, And
afterward receive me to glory. Psalm 73:24

*Every day will I bless thee; and I will praise
thy name for ever and ever. Psalm 145: 2*

Sing unto him, sing psalms unto him: talk
ye of all his wondrous works. Psalm 105:2

Let my heart be sound in thy statutes;
that I be not ashamed. Psalm 119:80

And now shall mine head be lifted up above mine enemies round
about me: therefore will I offer in his tabernacle sacrifices of joy;
I will sing, yea, I will sing praises unto the Lord. Psalm 27:6

The law of the LORD is perfect, converting the soul: the testimony of the LORD is sure, making wise the simple. Psalm 19:7

morning glory

*I will bless the Lord at all times: his praise shall
continually be in my mouth. Psalm 34:1*

prayer journal

By thee have I been holden up from the womb: thou art he that took me out of my mother's bowels: my praise shall be continually of thee. Psalm 71:6

Give unto the Lord the glory due unto his name; worship the Lord in the beauty of holiness. Psalm 29:2

*According to thy name, O God, so is thy praise unto the ends of
the earth: thy right hand is full of righteousness. Psalm 48:10*

He hath delivered my soul in peace from the battle that was against me: for there were many with me. Psalm 55:18

*I will praise the Lord according to his righteousness: and will
sing praise to the name of the Lord most high. Psalm 7:17*

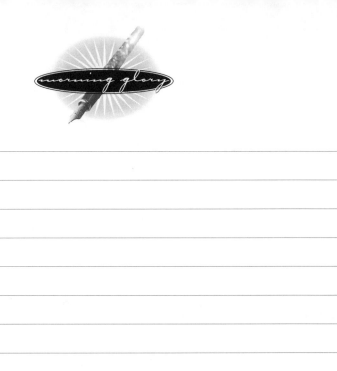

When thou saidest, Seek ye my face; my heart said
unto thee, Thy face, Lord, will I seek. Psalm 27:8

The humble shall see this, and be glad: and your
heart shall live that seek God. Psalm 69:32

But it is good for me to draw near to God: I have put my trust in the Lord God, that I may declare all thy works. Psalm 73:28

Other Books by Juanita Bynum

No More Sheets Hardback
No More Sheets Devotional
No More Sheets Quote Book
The Juanita Bynum Topical Bible
Morning Glory Devotional
Morning Glory Prayer Journal
Morning Glory Gift Book
Morning Glory Meditation Scriptures
Don't Get Off the Train
The Planted Seed
My Inheritance
Never Mess with a Man who Came Out of a Cave

Available at your local bookstore

Author Contact
Juanita Bynum Ministries
Post Office Box 939
Waycross, GA 31502
1-912-287-0032